Will You Be My Friend? is a sensitive collection of poetic reflections seeking to uncover the mysteries of love, loneliness, social and religious revolution, and, of course, friendship.

James Kavanaugh ponders the ease of making childhood friends and the gradual awareness that "friends are not so easy to find" as we move into adulthood and begin letting go of roles. He laments "this skinny little kid who never wanted to play tackle football at all but thought he'd better if he wanted his daddy to love him and to prove his courage. . . "; observes the loneliness prevalent among "people walking in the crowded streets, mumbling to themselves the words they will not share, and fearing that no one can understand the pain—or care"; revels in the loss of the judgmental God of childhood faith who "kept careful toll of all the deeds of men. . . with some black and lusting kind of pen"; expresses his admiration not for "heroes and celebrities or public martyrs whose deeds are properly recorded. . . " but for "the middle aged lady who. . . goes home alone to a little apartment where virginity is a cold fact and not a jewel in anyone's crown." Realizing that "revolution in history has seldom been fun," the poet challenges: "Let's revolutionize revolution! . . . free it from anger and force, make it a three-credit course." He seriously contemplates "I wish I were a planet so my sadness would have seasons. If it came with sun or snow, I'd somehow know its reasons." Then balancing it with humor he writes: "My pastor is a reverent soul who talks of love and homes. He seldom seems to lose control until he quotes Dow-Jones."

Will You Be My Friend? moves into larger themes of love and friendship. Kavanaugh fears that "maybe love is only a convenience that binds man and woman in comfort and economic exchange"; decries the lover who insists "love must never make demands" by responding "Would you talk to my heart sometime? He doesn't understand!" In a rare and extraordinary vision, the poet describes his experience of the fullness of love: "As I loved you, I loved all that loved you, and with the love given, even weakly, there appeared some endless quantity of love merging into circular ecstasy without evidence of start or finish." He finds joy in the light side of friendship: "We've got to stop laughing like this— someone might see us and wonder why we're still giggling when the whole world is weeping"; and finally returns to the fundamental issue as revealed in the title poem: "Will you be my friend? There are so many reasons why you never should: often I'm too serious, seldom predictably the same, sometimes cold and distant, probably I'll always change. . . . Will you be my friend? For no reason that I know except I want you so."

Will You Be My Friend? speaks out about love and friendship with the honesty and directness for which Kavanaugh is best known. Together with its predecessor, *There Are Men Too Gentle To Live Among Wolves*, these two classics have warmed the hearts of well over a million readers and are now available for the first time in softcover.

Will You
Be My Friend?

JAMES KAVANAUGH

Illustrations by
Marjorie Luy

ARGONAUT
PUBLISHING

DISTRIBUTED BY

HARPER & ROW
SAN FRANCISCO

WILL YOU
BE MY FRIEND?

For information address:
Argonaut Publishing
A Subsidiary of Crooked Angel Productions, Inc.
P.O. Box 189
Nevada City, CA 95959-0189

Distributed by
Harper & Row, Pub., Inc.
1700 Montgomery St.
San Francisco, CA 94111

Hardback Published by
Dutton - Sunrise, Inc.,
a subsidiary of E.P. Dutton
ISBN 0-87690-166-6 (hard)

Library of Congress Cataloging in Publication Data
Kavanaugh, James J.
  Will you be my friend?
  1. Friendship—Poetry. I. Title.
PS3561.A88W5   1984   811'.54   84-28291
ISBN 0-918777-01-1 (soft)

84 85 86 87 88 10 9 8 7 6 5 4 3 2 1

Printed in U.S.A.
First Softback Edition

Other Books by James Kavanaugh

Man in Search of God
A Modern Priest Looks at His Outdated Church
The Birth of God
The Struggle of the Unbeliever
The Crooked Angel
Between Man and Woman
There Are Men Too Gentle To Live Among Wolves
Faces in the City
Celebrate the Sun
America
Sunshine Days and Foggy Nights
Winter Has Lasted Too Long
Walk Easy on the Earth
A Coward for Them All
A Fable
Maybe If I Loved You More
Laughing Down Lonely Canyons

To you

Who have lived long enough
to hear your own voice,

Who will continue to search
even if you never find,

Who will only settle for love!

INTRODUCTION

LONELY PEOPLE WEEPING

PLIABLE PEOPLE

SADNESS HAS NO SEASONS

NO LIMITS TO MY DREAMING

WILL YOU
BE MY FRIEND?

Who am I? I am not sure.
Once I was a rabbit's grave and a basketball hoop on the garage, a cucumber patch, lilac trees and peonies crawling with ants. I was stepping stones and a mysterious cistern, grass fires, water fights and ping pong in the basement. I was a picket fence, a bed and maple chest of drawers I shared with brothers, a dog named Sandy who danced. Friends were easy to find. We climbed trees, built grass huts, chased snakes—and we dreamed a lot.
> WILL YOU BE MY FRIEND? Beyond childhood.

Who am I? I am not sure.
Once I was predictable. I was educated, trained, loved—not as I was, but as I seemed to be. My role was my safe way of hiding. There was no reason to change. I was approved. I pleased. Then, almost suddenly, I changed. Now I am less sure, more myself. My role has almost disappeared. My roots are not in my church, my job, my city; even my world. They are in me. Friends are not so easy to find—and I dream a lot.
> WILL YOU BE MY FRIEND? Beyond roles.

Who am I? I am not sure.
I am more alone than before. Part animal, but not protected by his instincts or restricted by his vision. I am part spirit as well, yet scarcely free, limited by taste and touch and time—yearning for all of life. There is no security. Security is sameness and fear, the postponing of life. Security is expectations and commitments and premature death. I live with uncertainty. There are mountains yet to climb, clouds to ride, stars to explode, and friends to find. I am all alone. There is only me— and I dream a lot.
> WILL YOU BE MY FRIEND? Beyond security.

Who am I? I am not sure.
I do not search in emptiness and need, but in increasing
fullness and desire. Emptiness seeks any voice to fill a void,
any face to dispel darkness. Emptiness brings crowds and
shadows easy to replace. Fullness brings a friend, unique,
irreplaceable. I am not as empty as I was. There are the wind
and the ocean, books and music, strength and joys within, and
the night. Friendship is less a request than a celebration, less a
ritual than a reality, less a need than a want. Friendship is you
and me—and I dream a lot.
WILL YOU BY MY FRIEND? Beyond need.

Who am I? I am not sure.
Who are you? I want to know.
We didn't sell Kool-aid together or hitchhike to school. We're
not from the same town, the same God, hardly the same world.
There is no role to play, no security to provide, no commitment
to make. I expect no answer save your presence, your eyes, your
self. Friendship is freedom, is flowing, is rare. It does not need
stimulation, it stimulates itself. It trusts, understands, grows,
explores, it smiles and weeps. It does not exhaust or cling,
expect or demand. It is—and that is enough—and it dreams a
lot.
WILL YOU BE MY FRIEND?

James Kavanaugh
Leucadia, California 1971

LONELY PEOPLE
WEEPING . . . .

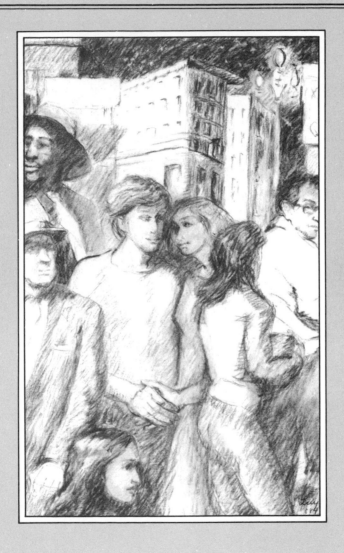

LONELY PEOPLE
WEEPING

Tonight I saw the people
Walking in the crowded streets,
Mumbling to themselves
The words they will not share,
And fearing that no one
Can understand the pain—or care.
Satisfied to find a home
Where someone knows their name,
Tasting their transcendence
In a weekly poker game
Or a lamp and yellow chair
That always seem the same.

Tonight I saw the people
Walking in the crowded streets,
Walking in the privacy of fog damp darkness,
Separate shadows apart,
Weary of step and heart,
Hands brushing, barely touching enough
To warm the fingers.
Tightly I held your hand,
Locking wrists amid the traffic noise,
And as I pulled you close, I heard
The lonely people weeping for their toys. 𝒬

I SAW
THE WORLD TODAY

I saw the world today
 Like a bloated body lying on the shore of space
 Dressed in white with a cincture of freeways,
 The lusting planets lapping coldly at his legs,
 His face furrowed with dry river beds,
 His hair disheveled like a burnt-out jungle,
 His cheeks brown and bruised like bloodless mountains,
While men with solemn faces tore at him like maggots
And women made shawls and slipcovers from his robes.

So I waited there
 For a man from Galilee or somewhere to walk on space,
 To shout above cascading comets and angry planets:
 "Lazarus come forth!"
 But the only voice was that of children laughing
  in the distance.
 Then the body rose and shook the maggots off,
 His face like the blinding sun, his hair like
  shining wheat,
 His garments gleamed like freshly fallen snow
  in moonlight,
As triumphantly he turned and said:
"I think I hear the children!" ✒

I WONDER

I wonder if the waves get weary
  With the salt and surfers on their backs,
Or if the wind is angry when
  It throws the rain against my windows?
I wonder if the mountains are lonely,
  Or only aloof,
If the desert is as sullen as it seems,
  Or only sad?
I wonder if the gulls are sick of eating fish,
If the sandpipers don't get tired of dodging waves?

Maybe we could send a man from earth
  To study the stress on the waves,
  To chart the temper of the wind
  And the temperament of the mountains,
  To tell the desert jokes until the sage
      shakes with laughter,
  To feed the gulls a balanced diet
      with mineral supplements,
  And the sandpipers? Well, tune them in to TV
  To hear the future of the tides.

I wonder funny things—like:
      "Do sandcrabs live in condominiums?" 🖎

I KNEW
THIS KID

I knew this skinny little kid
   Who never wanted to play tackle football at all
But thought he'd better if he wanted
   His daddy to love him and to prove his courage
And things like that.
   I remember him holding his breath
And closing his eyes
   And throwing a block into a guy twice his size,
Proving he was brave enough to be loved, and crying softly
   Because his tailbone hurt
And his shoes were so big they made him stumble.

I knew this skinny little kid
   With sky-blue eyes and soft brown hair
Who liked cattails and pussy willows. .
   Sumac huts and sassafras,
Who liked chestnuts and pine cones and oily walnuts,
   Lurking foxes and rabbits munching lilies,
Secret caves and moss around the roots of oaks,
   Beavers and muskrats and gawking herons.
And I wonder what he would have been
   If someone had loved him for
Just following the fawns and building waterfalls
   And watching the white rats have babies.
I wonder what he would have been
   If he hadn't played tackle football at all. ✎

MRS. FIXER

We call her Mrs. Fixer because she fixes
   Everything for everybody.
If you need a ride, you call her,
   Or a meal, or a telephone committee.
She'll find you an apartment or a part-time job,
   Even a date if you're in the market.
And all the time she only wants someone to love her
      But she's afraid to ask.

So she fixes everything for everybody instead
And you keep calling her when you need something
   And forget to tell her that you love her.
So she'll probably die lonely
   And have a big funeral
And everyone will tell about
   The way she fixed things all the time. ✑

THE
POST OFFICE

I've never dealt with Russian commissars
Nor spent a single day in prison camps,
But I often meet the ghost of buried czars
When I try to buy a roll of eight-cent stamps.
Post offices reek of government and death,
Of barren tables, somber pens on chains,
Of endless lines and agents short of breath,
Whose voices sound like just before it rains.

While fish markets have a style—and smell unique,
And even banks give plates and cups away.
Grocery clerks don't mumble when they speak,
But postal clerks are tutored in delay.
The postage stamps are hidden carefully in drawers,
And postage's never owed—by God it's *due!*
Tiles of subway brown are on the floors,
The decor smacks of early twine and glue.
But pictures give a touch of rare relief,
—The vintage shots of hunted, wanted ones—
They give me new respect for federal thieves
And reveries of robberies and guns,
Which sometimes seem to ease my rising stress
And help me think of bold, exciting days
When mail was borne on pony-back express,
Or Jesse James the reason for delays.

But as I wait in line amid the gloom,
—And agents leave for lunch when I get near—
My eyes attend the drab and stuffy room
And wonder what could possibly bring cheer.

Do you think wallpaper would help? ✒

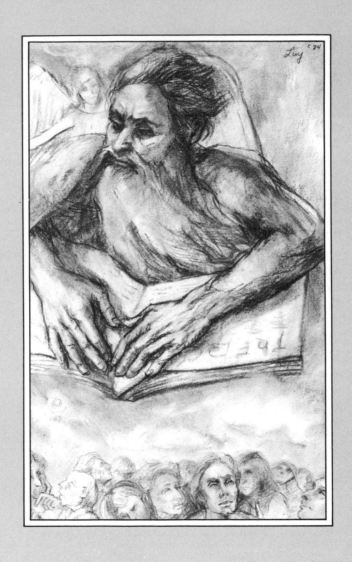

ONCE
I BELIEVED

Once I believed some gray and giant judge
Kept careful toll of all the deeds of men,
That with some black and lusting kind of pen
He cautiously recorded every petty crime
　　And most of all—
　　Mine!

Now I know there is no judge with righteous pen
Who bothers keeping track of deeds and time,
For every face records what life has been about
And sculpts a memory with every crack and line,
　　And most of all—
　　Mine! ❧

WELFARE
DOLES

One thing God should never do
  Is answer anyone's prayers.
If He answered but a single prayer,
  He wouldn't be God anymore,
But King of the Welfare Doles! 🦢

AVENGING
THE EARTH

The bulldozers are out in all their primitive fury
Like frothing metal monsters with steel claws
    and crunching jaws, prehistoric beasts reborn,
To avenge the earth which once destroyed them.
Ready like a Pharaoh's slaves to level mountains,
    fill the valleys and make straight the pathways
      of the kings,
To build a barracks for people of prefabricated dreams,
To build them row on row like crosses laid in Arlington
    or Flanders—a subtle symbol of life's sameness
      and the imminence of death,
To rip away the memories of earth's motion stored
    in mountains and to scatter sculpted monuments
      of sweating glaciers,
To push aside the wisdom of the wind and rain, and crush
    the contours shaped by time and the sensuous rhythm
      of nature's fondling,
To rip the shoulders from the hills, pull arms and legs
    from sockets, to gouge earth's eyes, to scar its face,
And claw away the furrows made by the flowing tears
    of spring and wonder,
To break its bones, tear out its hair, and peel away
    the skin until it is as tragic and faceless,
As docile and dull, as lifeless as the homes themselves
    and bland enough to build on.
Then to bring the plastic surgeons with artificial limbs
    and spongy breasts and straightened noses,
Their plastic and plaster, wire thread and transfusions,
Sperm banks and blood banks, their cuts and casts
    and sterile gowns, their drugs and anesthesia.

There is no music in the mortar nor magic in the hammer's
    drumming, hardly a place for craftsmen with only
Barracks to be assembled, camps and planned compounds,
    depots for the dispossessed and alien.
Love does not live in the walls nor in the air,
    only sameness.
Houses well content to find a plot flat enough
        to please the plumber, to satisfy the hungry builder
        and the computerized, avenging architect.
And when the earth is silent and the screams are gone,
When the groaning has ceased and salt is trampled
    in the ground,
When the fences are built with fear and pools
    filled with tears,
Then the tents are ready for the troops and man will
    tend his grass and tailored flowers
Where once there was carefree celebration.
Then the dozers drift away like death to build
        more burial sites, while Leviathan and brontosaurs,
        dictators and dinosaurs are avenged.
Man has made his mausoleum and will pay handsomely
    to rest there,
Assembled with other lonely men and women
    impatiently awaiting death! ✎

THE EARTHQUAKE CAME

One sullen day the earthquake came
To place the world among the planets,
Full of heat and rage and feebleness.
The earth sucked in her breath,
Sighed in discomfort,
And stretched her arms to ease the pent-up pain.
Man forgot payments and profits,
And, with new priorities, only remembered
To cling to his wife and children
As when the world was young,
For suddenly life was more than ritual or raiment.

The tall buildings swayed and moaned and begged
A drop of lamb's blood on the lintel
To keep away the earth's avenging angel,
While the little houses only shook and trembled.
The streets were filled with people
Hoping to find courage and comfort from those
They had scarcely noticed before when
Fear held them apart—until a greater fear
Dissolved the lesser one in longing.
And for a moment man could find
No place to lay his head
Save near his neighbor.

Amid the terror of the streets,
The rubbery rolling of the ground,
There was a gentleness and caring.
Then the earth settled back
Content to rest a little longer
And carry man against her bruised and ancient breast,
As when the world was young.

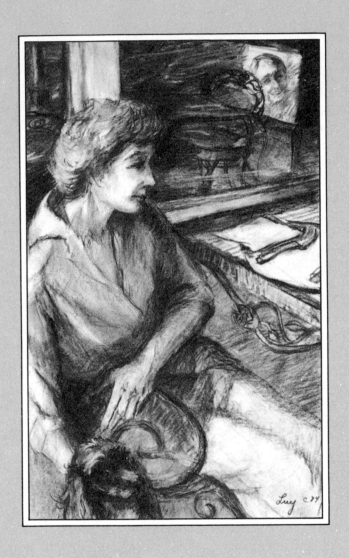

OF HEROES

I have never much admired heroes and celebrities
   or public martyrs
Whose deeds are properly applauded and whose vanity
   is warmed even behind bars.
Nor have I been much taken with chastity and celibacy
   and varied and sundry virginities.
My heart is moved by the middle-aged lady who walks
   her cat or curbs her dog in the early evening
And goes home alone to a little apartment
   where virginity is a cold fact
And not a jewel in anyone's crown,
Where martyrdom is not measured by white robes
   or assassination,
But by a single place setting and
   a lonely two-week vacation.

TERROR

You do not know who terror is
  But he is you—before you go to work,
  Gather children, caress your cat,
  Drink coffee, make love!
He is called "depression" or a "bad day,"
Gentle names to spirit him away. But he is terror.
  And he waits!

You do not know where terror is
  But he lives in dreams or early mornings,
  Behind eyes and ears,
  Behind rusty-hinged jaws
Even as they smile and whisper clichés
Instead of screaming at the days. But he is terror.
  And he waits!

One night he came to me
To rip away the cover
That I might see
  the seething spiders
  the tangled snakes
  the writhing worms of terror
Oozing up walls and under baseboards of my being.
I did not cry out"God!" but "Mother!"
And reaching for her hand to lead me from the dark,
  I found there was no hand. Only terror.
And he waits!

PLIABLE
PEOPLE....

THE
PLIABLE PEOPLE

The pliable people with the kind and frightened eyes
Are heading for Hawaii with its clear and friendly skies
With all good wishes from their children
   For fifteen days and fourteen nights of fun,
   Hula lessons, fruity drinks of rum,
   To gather shells and tan in tropic sun
   Or smilingly to pose in boldly colored clothes
   Authentically Hawaiian, and then to repartee
   With Art and Emily from Tennessee—
      Or was it Texas?

The pliable people with the kind and frightened eyes
Are heading for Hawaii with its clear and friendly skies
With all good wishes from their children
   To hear the pounding surf on Waikiki,
   To see the things a tourist's told to see,
   To purchase gifts—perhaps a bargain shroud—
   And when the mounting silence sounds too loud
   To laugh in leis or watch a midnight show,
   —And talk of friends who died a year ago—
      Or was it longer?

I know the days that molded them, I know
      how they were made,
For life was always just ahead, when mortgages were paid.
Security—the guarantee they'd always be afraid—
   Till suddenly they realized that life had passed them by.
   And even as I watch them and feel a sadness rise,
I love the pliable people with the kind and frightened eyes.

   Next year the Caribbean, indeed, indeed!
   Then perhaps Tahiti, God speed, God speed!

LIFE IS A
SALESMAN

Life is a salesman who sucks me in
  And flatters me for profit.
  He courts and fawns on me,
  Smiles a special smile,
  Knows my favorite wine and music,
  Laughs at my jokes,
  Applauds my insights—
Until I sign my name.
Then he deserts me and his secretary says,
  "Sorry—he's not available!"

MY
PROFESSIONAL HELPERS

My pastor is a reverent soul
  Who talks of love and homes,
He seldom seems to lose control
  Until he quotes Dow-Jones.

My doctor gives me medicine
  To still the hand of fate.
In speech he is quite reticent—till
  He talks of real estate.

My lawyer is a Lincoln fan
  With precedents quite rare,
His view of law and order, man,
  Is: "What"ll the traffic bear?"

Only my dentist seems to care,
  His drilling's a joy to behold.
My inlays he puts eternally there.
  Could the bastard be cornering gold?

WHEN FEAR SHOWS IN THE EYES
LOVERS SOON ARE GONE

When fear shows in the eyes, lovers soon are gone
And darkness comes too soon on winter nights in cities
Where a lonely lady loved a cat enough to feed him promptly
Save for nights she'd not come home at all
But stayed to love a stranger after drinks and waited
    for his call,
Then fed her cat again the more devotedly
And even slept with him the day before she died.
And in surprise the neighbors found her
Three days dead before they even knew.
Even the cat stopped pawing her in but a day or two
And whined for food from any hand at all, while mourners
    whispered:
"It was good that she died first since she was all alone," for
When fear shows in the eyes, lovers soon are gone!

When fear shows in the eyes, lovers soon are gone
And darkness comes too soon on winter nights in cities
Where ladies cling to cats, caressing them in lieu of lovers,
Feeding them, or gently fondling them beneath the covers
On cold and lonely nights, or trailing them along the streets,
Their frowning mouths too frightened to be softened
    by a kiss,
Like prisoners bound by barbed wire lips, held captive
By the concrete chins that won't give in to screams or even
    trembling,
Searching eyes like floodlights in the skies
    —ladies led on leashes—
Pulling mufflers close enough to warm the life that's left,
Struggling hard to hold the strand of stretching leather
Lest they only have themselves and no other—for
When fear shows in the eyes, lovers soon are gone!

THE SOLEMN
PSYCHOLOGIST

The voice of the solemn psychologist
  Droned in its studied control,
A velvet overdrive with the
  Well-lubricated meshing of tearless gears,
Homeostatic acceleration from zero to zero
  All in seconds,
Talking dispassionately about passion
  And turning anger into petulance,
Explaining rage and rape, anguish and broken hearts
  In esoteric and bloodless words.
And when I finally said: "Urinations on you, little man!"
  He smiled and asked: "Was your father overbearing?"

REVOLUTION

Revolution in history has seldom been fun.
It's a story of sadness, the way it's been done.
The Minutemen slaughtered and bloodied up fate,
And Waterloo wisdom came centuries late.
   Too late? That's hate!

Let's revolutionize revolution,
Make it a permanent institution,
Free it from blood and contusions,
Provide it with happy transfusions,
   And call it our national sport!

The Prussians and Russians revolted with guns,
And pompous old Rome was too cruel with the Huns.
The wandering Moslems liked blood with their sod,
The Jews and the Christians both murdered for God.
   For God? That's odd!

Let's revolutionize revolution!
Make it a permanent institution,
Free it from anger and force,
Make it a three-credit course,
   And call it our national sport! ❦

THE
FAMILY ALBUM

Childhood seems so long ago
  With faces dim, forgotten names,
And special friends I used to know,
  The camping trips and softball games,
The lonely times and longing dreams,
  The Sunday Church and Tarzan show.

Childhood seems so long ago,
  some other world I used to know,
Some other ocean's ebb and flow
  Until the family albums show:
    Some sad and sensitive boy—
      With a space between his teeth—
      Staring at me. 𝄢

THE
SCHIZOPHRENIC

Lonely schizophrenic, your self is split in two,
Even brothers wonder, just which of them is you.
Now I've a different problem, I've lately recognized,
When I try to be myself, I've thirteen different sides.

Lover
Hater
Trusting as a lamb,
  Idealist
  Realist
  Dirty old man.
Falstaffian, philosopher,
Ascetic as a monk,
  Elfish, selfish,
A sometimes rowdy drunk!

Let's see—that's twelve of me,
  There has to be another.
Ah yes! The failure
  That disappointed mother.

Lucky schizophrenic, I find I envy you,
When you try to be yourself, you're only split in two. 🖋

TO LOSE
A FRIEND

It's hard to lose a friend, to know
  In some sudden awareness,
  In an instant's intuition
That you've been used, perhaps unconsciously
  In subtle strategy,
  In cautious calculation.
A friend dissolves before your very eyes
  In preposterous transformation,
  In macabre metamorphosis.
Suddenly the hands grow slimy that once felt strong,
Mucilage forms around the mouth and turns to slush,
  But it's mostly in the eyes!
They used to beam somehow—but now they're red and ratlike.
And their silvery sparkle of love and warmth becomes
  The beadiness of dull, gray marbles.
Words ring hollow, the face seems puffed,
  But it's mostly in the eyes.
Memories are little stabs around the heart.
  It's hard to lose a friend! 🖋

ONCE A LAD

Once a lad with untold eagerness for love and life
And questions in his eyes for which there were no words,
With energy like freshly bubbling springs emerging
      from the ground,
Made his way to silent groves in academe and found
A grammarian's gravity to tell of Caesar and Homer
In words without surprise, dim and dull,
Replete with rules, insisting that Achilles was
      but a genitive attending "heel"
And Agamemnon proper subject of a sentence hardly real.
The blood was parsed from books, poetry lost
      in ponderous prose,
Reading but a rat's performance memorized by those
Who fought for little pellets of A's or B's
And heard grave warnings made to boys who felt
      the breeze of Troy
Or made a hero of Hannibal on his elephants
When masters bade him trudge across snowy Alps,
Only to lead a verb again in search of its object.

The lad became a kind of man replete with scholar's
      expertise that seemed to promise love,
But offered testimonials instead, and left him filled
With anguish and emptiness, disgust for learning,
A seething desire to hang a collection of his masters
Until the blood flowed from their infinitives and tenses,
And their flesh could modify the ground in search
      of all their senses!

Stupid lad! You should have known! A single glance enough:
Gray buildings with bilious yellow halls, no music calls
Or flowers, only Spartan sundries, clean terrazzo floors
That merely seemed like stone but tasted lean
   like disinfectant and cement,
Barren bathrooms, waxen toilet paper, beds aligned
   like coffins,
Windows without curtains like prying eyes, the air dead,
Food pale and pasty, unloved, a desperate creation where
Potatoes disappeared in a milky, motherless incarnation.

God! He hated creamed potatoes sliding down his throat!
A proper pall for those who managed to endure it all,
Hoping that after battle there would appear some gentle,
   loving face to hold the weary warrior
In a nurturing embrace. But alas! Too late! Hope was only
Fantasy of heaven or release from stress, and passion
Squeezed like grapes was turned to vinegar's success.

And oh, the sallow cheeks that checked his every move,
Making it tense and angular till nothing round survived.
Circles made no sense amid triangular and esoteric gods.
But most of all a lad who wanted love, a reason to laugh,
And got instead a scholar's rules and daily duels to
   break a spirit
Till he cried, "I will not die!" but tried so hard
And such momentum built to stay alive that even now
   He only struggles badly to survive,
   And not to choke upon a single memory of
    Silence and soberness,
    Discipline and somberness,
And creamed potatoes sliding down his throat. ❧

SADNESS
HAS NO SEASONS....

MY SADNESS
HAS NO SEASONS

My sadness has no seasons,
It comes when the leaves
   Surrender to the persistent wind
   And lie at attention,
When the snow
   Coats twigs and footprints
   In a gentle obituary of white,
Or when the birds
   Fly back to the parks
   To help the old folks count the years.
It even comes when the hot air
   Keeps the crickets awake,
   Complaining in the parched grass.

There are no reasons for my sadness
   Except living, and maybe dying.
But mostly it moves in like the fog,
Seeping from some secret cave where shadows live.

I wish I were a planet so my sadness would have seasons,
If it came with sun or snow, I'd somehow know its reasons.

A GURU

I want a guru of my own!
I don't want to try him. I want to buy him.
And hang him in a closet in my home.
  I don't demand the Maharishi—I'll accept a lesser species
But I've got to have a guru of my own.
  I want to wear a toga and put sandals on my feet,
  I want to live with Yoga, unconcerned with what I eat.
I'm tired of competition and the noisy human voice,
I can't afford tuition on the island of my choice.
I can't survive the city with its crowded streets and gloom,
If some guru won't take pity and join me in my room.
I don't want to try him. I want to buy him.
And spend the day together chanting "OMMMMM!"

ONE SUNDAY AFTERNOON

One Sunday afternoon
You saw my tears
   Precipitous and sobbing from my eyes,
Too fierce to be ashamed,
Too wounded to be stealthy,
Too sudden to be announced,
And while the water washed your hands and face
   You held me close
To siphon out the pain.

One Sunday afternoon
You saw my tears
   And like an anxious mother asked:
"What brings such weeping?"
   And even as you asked for reasons
The torrents dissappeared.
   Only stains of tears remained.

What do reasons have to do with tears?

IN THE
CLEARING

Alone in the clearing stood the curious doe
To startle me as aimlessly I drove
Along a road and stopped to study her
Now motionless and staring without fright
As if protected by the now declining light of dusk
And begging freedom from the sight of subdivided land
And sprawling, country homes.

She boldly stared, now well aware that June
Is when the flowers grow and summer's sun
Brings respite from the hunter and his gun.
With ears still held in readiness to run,
Made anxious by the hungry real estate
That fences pasture land where once she ate,
She must rely on signals from her mate
Who watches at the nearby water site
Where only oily frogs dare sing of life
Or brash mosquitoes, emboldened by the silent birds,
Harass the last remaining herds
And hum their pesky song to warn the doe
That night will soon undress the moon to lure the trees,
To whisper secret love words in the breeze.

But then, as if I alone had caused the hurt,
She stirred and gently lifted up her skirt,
While branding me a bold, outrageous flirt,
And picked her way among the rocks and limbs
To join a gentler mate, and then to wait
To bed with him in warmth when darkness comes—
Expecting fall and angry men with guns.

THE LONELY ONES
ARE PHONING ME TODAY

The lonely ones are phoning me today
Using any pretext to camouflage the emptiness and fear,
Some cheery good news to hide the silence of a heart
Grown as gray as this sullen day on the ocean
When gulls and sand blend with the motion
Of the surf—and life seems only this:
　　Solemn submission to loneliness!

The lonely ones are phoning me today
Asking the word that no one can say,
To ease the hurt of love that's lost,
Children gone, or dreams that died,
Running from the word that echoes inside:
　　"Alone! I'm alone!
　　No one to share!
　　Alone! I'm all alone!
　　No one to care!"

The lonely ones are phoning me today,
Tired of the cat and composure, bored with bourbon,
Hiding their pain in synthetic questions
Just to hear a voice, a laugh, a bit of hope,
To play the game until the bleeding stops
And time takes hold, or anger, or courage.
　　Or maybe love.
When life seems more than this:
　　Solemn submission to loneliness! ✎

MAYBE LOVE

Maybe love is only a convenience that binds man and woman
  In comfort and economic exchange,
A subtle barter blessed by God, caressed by time and
      circumstance,
  A plot that cowards have arranged,
A kind of clinging to keep hands from trembling
  And hearts from knowing loneliness and pain.
Maybe love is only a convenience
  To fill a void called endlessness,
  To give structure to emptiness,
  To give a name to nothingness.

Maybe there is no love, maybe it's all an investment,
      a game of mirrors,
An ego reflecting itself in cautious and progressive calculation,
Maybe love is only a surrender of power
  To wound and waste me,
  To send me searching for sanity in the night's silence,
  To tear at my stomach, to fill me with choking tears—
  Too frozen to flow, too angry to spill—
  To leave me hopeless and helpless and sobbing to the wind,
Then to call me back and offer solace from the anguish
      love itself produced.

Love! Let me alone! I don't want some dutiful commitment
  To attend me until I am a corpse,
Some devout and generous self annihilation in my behalf.
Love! Go martyr yourself somewhere else!
Choose your victims form the weary and forlorn!
  I still have the wind—and sea—and me!🖊

I LOST YOU—
SOMEWHERE AMONG THE MARTINIS

I lost you—somewhere among the martinis—
You drifted off in gin-mist, distilled euphoria.
   Why didn't you stay?
   I wanted you! I needed you!
I know it's hard, to live that is.
But why did you run away?
   We were going to hurt together.
   Remember?
   To be real when all else was artifact.

Later you put your arms around me
And a voice that sounded like yours
   Groaned with pleasure as we made love.
But I was sad because I lost you
   Somewhere among the martinis!

OF WHALES
AND TAILS

Skyscrapers and spacerockets
Tend to leave me cold,
Man can walk upon the moon
To gather dust like gold
And I am only bored.
Seven-forty-sevens just make a bigger roar,
And fancy homes are gaudy tombs—
Really nothing more.
Quite easily ignored.

But tell me that a whale
Will flip his mighty tail
Or a fat iguana's lying on the sand,
I can spend a day
With the porpoises at play
Or watching honkers heading for the land.
I'm one who loves what lives,
I take to things that grow.
Moonrockets bore me silly,
But I'm awed by a feeding doe.

And lately love, I look at you,
Like a porpoise in the sea,
Your exquisite tail
Like the wandering whale
Is really too much for me.
You are my fat iguana,
My gently feeding doe,
You are the goose that turns me loose,
So, need I tell you more?

DO NOT
DISTURB

I will not pay homage to the bargain women
　　make with men,
A home and leisure for a little girl's petulance,
To amuse myself in a schoolboy's fantasy
While she protects her puberty like some proud princess,
Open to any juggler or jester who chances by,
Closed to me, unless I play a childhood game of
"Pokey on the icebox!"

Well fie on it! Aroint thee! Avaunt!
Keep your precious dowry of stiffened hair and
　　frozen fluids
That only flow in union with the flimsy freedom born of
Novelty or comfort—never in spontaneity or surprise.
If you can't love with your body, who can trust your heart
That hangs like a motel door screaming to a houseboy:
"Do not disturb!"

I want one whose arms are earthy enough to melt,
Whose mouth blends with her cheeks,
Whose breasts are not citadels but flowing fountains.
Or should I wait for forty years, wait till rust and ravage
Turn tempestuous desire into the breezes of senility,
Where aged arms hold each other up and withered faces
Have sacrificed their wit and wisdom to look alike.

If this be love, if such time it takes to flow
Like streams over rocks and through meadows
Until the rocks are chalky and dry and the meadows gray,
Then I will hire a charwoman to hold me up
And the face I see at eighty may have some semblance
To the one I knew at eighteen! 🖎

I DON'T KNOW
WHEN

I don't know when it was
   Your flesh became like mine
To touch—to taste—to see,
   And when I saw your face,
I somehow saw my own!

Nor do I know when it was
   Your flesh became alien
To touch—to taste—to see,
   And when I saw your face,
I somehow saw a stranger!

SOME DAY

Some day I'll walk away
    And be free
And leave the sterile ones
    Their secure sterility.
I'll leave without a forwarding address
And walk across some barren wilderness
    To drop the world there.
    Then wander free of care
Like an unemployed Atlas.

SO MUCH
I WANTED TO SAY

There was so much I wanted to say
But it got lost among recipes and yesterday's movies
And all the things that strangers talk about
   To keep the silence from ticking too loud.
Our different worlds met in the night
And waved as we went by—each leaning on our axis—
Each surrounded by a different set of stars,
   Even a separate moon.
We were children last night—
   Begging a parent to look and see
While we did somersaults to please,
Looking for the word or smile that said: "You're loved!"
I woke this morning with futility and loneliness
Wondering if there could ever rise that moment of joy,
   Or if my very being made it impossible.
Perhaps the Christians are right—
   Self-sacrifice is back in style,
Perhaps man has no right to be himself,
   To find love in the night.
But I have known love—
Known moments when my very giving
   Was as spontaneous as the sunlight.
Then followed other times.
But they will pass,
   And love will come again. ✑

NO LIMITS
TO MY DREAMING....

ONCE
THERE WERE

Once there were
  No limits to my dreaming
  No boundaries to my ambitions
  No love I could not possess.
Some fire raged within
  Volcanic and seething
  Nourished by success
  That only at intervals could rest.
Each day another test,
Each idea a challenge beyond compromise,
Critics only shadows, empty voices
  That came and went.
Then I lost a love I thought I owned
And tried to conquer life myself alone
While age came crashing into youth
  In cosmic conflict,
And left me lost in fears I'd never known.

So now I'd like
  To kiss your hand
  Maybe laugh a bit
  Give a flower life
  Love a child.
Then again there would be
  No limits to my dreaming!

LAST NIGHT'S
LOVE

I wonder if last night's love was silent
  Because words would have interfered,
Or if our silence only told
  Of private fantasies too secretive to share?
Our eyes did not meet, only our cheeks,
  Rubbing like boats tied patiently to drying docks
Awaiting some joyous footstep to give them life.

  I wonder if last night's love was silent
Because words would have interfered,
  Or if like children we had drifted off
To private worlds where there is touching and tasting,
  Laughing and whispering and sworn secrets
And music and sunlight on rootbeer rivers.

SOMEONE
MIGHT SEE US

We've got to stop laughing like this—
    Someone might see us
And wonder why we're still giggling
    When the whole world is weeping.
(Did I tell you
    That you have a clown's face,
That your ears are too big for your head,
    Poking through your hair
Like curious children,
    Begging to be nibbled at?)
But we've got to stop laughing like this
    With tears in our eyes
(Which is a nice way for tears to take their leave).
    Someone might see us
And wonder why we're still laughing
    When the evening news
Only permits an occasional grin.
    (Did I tell you that
Your bottom lip hangs down
    Like a baby bulldog's,
That your teeth are crooked
    And I love you?)
But we've got to stop laughing like this
    And get some goals—or be practical
And maybe save the world because
    Someone might see us
And wonder why we're laughing
    When the bankers look worried and money's tight
(Did I tell you that your nose is bent,
    That you have hound's eyes
And squirrel's cheeks
    And I love you?)🐿

A FLEETING
VISION

One day, For some reason known only to the gods
Who understand the motion of the planets,
　　　The mystery of the stars,
There came suddenly and fleetingly to me
A burst of love unlike any feeling I had ever known
That it grew like some mystic fire around my heart
And warmed the secret crevices where ego disappears.
I did not call it forth, it came, nor will I ever
Be the same even if the vision never comes again.
I did not love at all, but rather I was by love itself
Possessed. And death joined life in a mysterious merging
As if my vast and loving letting go made some contact
With the motion of the universe, as if some secret harmony
Hidden from me before was now as obvious as the wind,
And each pulsing heart was but a feeble echo
Of some universal beating of man or animal or tempest.

It was a love as sensual as it was mystical, as sexual
As it was transcendant, the world and I were one.
You were sleeping and I when I touched your breast
My hand contained the strength and softness of every
Human heart and asked that life might be my friend
And let me love him, only giving what flows from motion
　　　Shared with stars and planets.
And as I loved you, I loved all that loved you,
And with the love given even weekly, there appeared some
Endless quantity of love merging into circular ecstasy
Without evidence of start or finish. Death did not hold
Angry dominion over life like an impatient landlord
Waiting to exact his payment. And when you softly said,
"I love you" your voice was mine as well
　　　And every voice proclaiming "Love!"

Mystics and prophets blanched before the message
       Of life itself,
Redemption rolled in with the waves stretched out
Like giant lips endlessly kissing the shore
As if to melt in eternal longing.
The ocean's roaring cadence shouted "Love,"
Clouds grew out of the horizon's grayness
Into billowing, blushing maidens adorned by the sun,
Attending the loving union of sea and land.
Sandpipers strutted down to taste the ocean's offerings,
Shells crawled upon the land to merge their bodies
       With the golden sand.
Suddenly there was time enough to love!
There was no you or I, but only all, each measured
By the motion of his heart, the rhythm of his flowing.
Each human quest a secret search for the pulsing of life.

Microcosm merged with macrocosom to join
The harmony of the universe. And as I gazed at you,
Each scar upon your body was a memory of life,
Ancient as marks on mountains, young as infant's crying.
Do not cast me from you life, my love, you are my entrance
To mysteries which poets stumble to express and libraries
Repeat like weary mouths with fast decaying teeth.
My vision drifted off as quickly as it came,
Sadness settled like sudden fog, to make the ocean quieter,
More profound, readying itself for a later burst of light.

And when the night has come to calm my heart and join it
With the phantoms of the dark, I will not sleep to calm
The vision's violence. My love, still too deep to express,
Like some waiting fault beneath the surface, which
If uttered all at once would crack the earth
And we would be dissolved in dust and trembling.

So love must speak in symbols,
A touch upon the head, a name, a pushing back of hair
More tender than the ocean's kisses,
Gentler than the west wind's brushing back the fronds
        Of patient palms.
This is enough of love!
Enough to hold you, to feel the mist of night
Enfold you in protective coolness.
Only rarely can I say "I love you,"
Lest I startle you with the giant, pulsing,
        Single heart of life.
The vision's memory is enough to keep my love intact,
To tell of love and life transcending time,
And join us in a marriage with the universe
Where death is only life
        When merged with love! ℚ

LOVE AND BREATH
BEYOND BELIEF

Love and life and breath beyond belief
And dreams all destined to be fulfilled,
   A heart too full to make sense,
   With giraffes dancing with kangaroos
   And songs lustier than a pumpkin moon,
   With dancing stars and every moment making love
   And bearing children too winsome to weep,
   A hand long enough to reach the heavens
   And to tickle them unti they can only giggle
   And shout delightedly:
"My God, it's beautiful! It's man!" ℞

SHE'S TOO PROSY
FOR ME

I met a girl more beautiful than you,
  Who's probably brighter—even more elegant,
But she's too prosy for me, and
    Moves in pages and paragraphs,
    Speaks in sentences,
    Lives in chapters
    With the commas all in place,
    Predictable and shorn of wonder.
Line flows coherently from line
    With logic and reason,
    With judgment and taste,
    With index and footnotes,
    with rules and rituals,
    The mystery's edited out.

Your are poetry to me
    Without rhyme or reason,
    Without systems or schedules,
    Without requirements and obligations,
    Or disappointments and expectations,
    God knows—without a watch!
Your sudden lines surprise me,
    Shy and startling,
    Bold and unafraid
    Of silence
    Or challenge—or change,
    Or repetition—or repetition!

You are poetry to me
   Like chili on a cold night with lots of crackers,
   Or eating Hershey bars in duckblinds,
   Or wandering through a market in Mexico.
I met a girl more beautiful than you,
But she could never look like someone I know
   Coming out of the rain
   In a canvas coat,
   A droopy hat,
And in sneakers—of all things! 🖋

EVERY TIME
I SEE YOU

Every time I see you
   The pain comes back again,
And my chest goes tight
   Somewhere around my heart.
I like the tension better
   When it's in my stomach,
So I can eat it away
   Or seduce it with martinis.
The chest pain is not seduceable,
   It only wants your arms
And that's impossible
   Because you told me
That love must never make demands.

Would you talk to my heart sometime?
   He doesn't understand! 🍃

GUADALAJARA

Guadalajara is
    Woman's love and all the softness of the world,
    Fragrance born beyond time,
        sensuality surrendering to laughter,
    A breeze wrapping lovers in silken sheets,
    A baby born to laugh and play
And not to turn away.

Guadalajara is
    A mother who takes time to love her children,
    A father without the pallor of premature death,
    A man who falls in love a hundred times a day,
    A woman with coffee eyes that linger
And do not turn away.

Guadalajara is the memory of war when
    Fathers killed their sons,
    Blood flowed on cobblestones,
    Slavery was the price of freedom.
Guadalajara is the memory of
    Lonely men who put away their guns,
    Lovers returning to the parks,
    And eyes that never turn away! ℚ

I CANNOT
LOOK AT YOU TODAY

I cannot look at you today,
Your eyes devour me
Not with the look of freedom and friendship,
But with the stare of omnivorous eating.
Your hunger is too great,
Your famine too fierce.
Your lips do not taste me now.
You are all teeth!
Your hot breath scalds me,
Your tongue is savage and swordlike,
You suckle to survive.
Your arms do not hold and caress,
But cling and claw
And tell me not so much you love me,
But that no one else should.

I feel no passion now—only gentleness.
Let me hold you, easy, like a child for a time,
And rouse in you the pride and power of your own being,
As grand and strong and beautiful as mine.
And do not hate me for what is not mine to give
Nor yours to take! 🖎

WILL YOU
BE MY FRIEND?

Will you be my friend?
There are so many reasons why you never should:
I'm sometimes sullen, often shy, acutely sensitive,
My fear erupts as anger, I find it hard to give,
I talk about myself when I'm afraid
And often spend a day without anything to say.
   But I will make you laugh
   And love you quite a bit
   And hold you when you're sad.
I cry a little almost every day
Because I'm more caring than the strangers ever know,
And, if at times, I show my tender side
(The soft and warmer part I hide)
   I wonder,
   Will you be my friend?
A friend
   Who far beyond the feebleness of any vow or tie
   Will touch the secret place where I am really I,
   To know the pain of lips that plead and eyes that weep,
   Who will not run away when you find me in the street
   Alone and lying mangled by my quota of defeats
But will stop and stay—to tell me of another day
When I was beautiful.

Will you be my friend?
There are so many reasons why you never should:
Often I'm too serious, seldom predictably the same,
Sometimes cold and distant, probably I'll always change.
I bluster and brag, seek attention like a child,
I brood and pout, my anger can be wild,
    But I will make you laugh
    And love you quite a bit
    and be near when you're afraid.
I shake a little almost every day
Because I'm more frightened than the strangers ever know
And if at times I show my trembling side
(The anxious, fearful part I hide)
    I wonder,
    Will you be my friend?
A friend
    Who, when I fear your closeness, feels me push away and
    Stubbornly will stay to share what's left on such a day,
    Who, when no one knows my name or calls me
            on the phone,
    When there's no concern for me—what I have
            or haven't done—
    And those I've helped and counted on have,
            oh so deftly, run,
    Who, when there's nothing left but me,
            stripped of charm and subtlety,
    Will nonetheless remain.

    Will you be my friend?
        For no reason that I know
        Except I want you so. ✑

ABOUT THE AUTHOR

James Kavanaugh is the author of more than twenty books of philosophy, psychology, theology, fiction, and poetry. One of seven sons of an Irish-Catholic family, he was ordained, but left the priesthood in 1968 after his explosive *A Modern Priest Looks At His Outdated Church* ignited an ongoing revolution in the Catholic Church. The following year he began writing poetry, and, in 1970, published his first collection of poems, *There Are Men Too Gentle To Live Among Wolves.* A bestseller, it marked the beginning of a long line of popular poetic collections to come. This prolific author's most recent volumes of poetry include *Maybe If I Loved You More* and *Laughing Down Lonely Canyons;* the spring of 1985 will see the release of his latest fiction, *The Celibates.*

James Kavanaugh is truly "the poet of the American people," as Abigail Van Buren ("Dear Abby") has so aptly called him. He was one of nine artists recently invited by the Chinese government to share his reflections on the American way of life with audiences in Peking and Shanghai.

He is a man of many talents and accomplishments. While holding a Ph.D. in Religious Philosophy from Catholic University of America in Washington, D.C., Kavanaugh also became a licensed Clinical Psychologist and Marriage and Family Counselor in California. He travels throughout America and Canada holding workshops, lecturing at numerous universities, and giving poetry readings that move people to laughter, to tears, to experiencing the world more fully.

James Kavanaugh wanders the byways of California from the northern Sierra foothills to the southern coast, directing the Institute which bears his name. Kavanaugh feels the Institute grew out of the public's response to the release of *There Are Men Too Gentle To Live Among Wolves.* In the Introduction, his words signaled the emergence of a new group of people in the seventies: men and women seeking to become all they can be. James Kavanaugh defined this new sensibility when he declared himself to be a *searcher;* since then, countless people have contacted him to announce that they are *searchers* too, sharing in the quest he so eloquently interprets and so compellingly challenges others to join. He comments, "Now, fifteen years and thousands of requests later, I have established the *James Kavanaugh Institute* for *searchers*. It is a haven where men and women in such painful transitions as divorce or death, aging or self-doubt, or even the awareness that life is passing them by, can meet with kindred spirits. There they find loving support, new insights, and fresh energy in Search Workshops that develop the principles of growth that have directed me in my personal odyssey. . . . When the Retreat Center is completed, and I can provide the healthy, joyful, loving environment that people need for total healing, my dream of fifteen years will be fulfilled." Through the Institute, some of the Kavanaugh poetry is available in cards, cassettes, and LP recordings. For more information regarding Search Workshops, out-of-print books, or any of the above items, contact:

The James Kavanaugh Institute
116 E. De La Guerra
Santa Barbara, CA 93101

ABOUT THE ILLUSTRATOR

Marjorie Luy is a painter. She can be counted among the few who have truly dedicated their lives to painting. In the early years, she had tender guidance from the renowned New York artist, Phillip Guston, as well as from many others who gave her inspiration and encouragement. After graduating from the Cranbrook Academy of Art in Michigan, she pursued her main interest: painting the face and human figure with its grace, beauty, and psychological undertones. This led her to the island of Bali in 1975 where she felt fortunate to find all these qualities in the tiny dancers.

For the past twenty eight years, she has made Santa Barbara her home where she paints in a studio built by her husband, Bill. Her work has earned acclaim through numerous gallery exhibitions and acquisitions by private collectors.